Olivia Rodrigo: The Ultimate Fan Book

100+ Olivia Rodrigo Facts, Photos, Quiz + More

Jenny Kellett

BELLANOVA

MELBOURNE · SOFIA · BERLIN

Copyright © 2022 Jenny Kellett

Sofia, Bulgaria 1st Edition: 29 June, 2022

Olivia Rodrigo: The Ultimate Fan Book

www.bellanovabooks.com

ISBN: 978-619-92219-0-7

All Images Licensed for Editorial Use By **Shutterstock.com**.

All rights reserved. No part of this book may be reproduced in any form by any electronic or mechanical means including photocopying, recording, or information storage and retrieval without permission in writing from the author.

Olivia Rodrigo was not involved in the writing of this book. However, all facts are believed to be truthful based on reputable, public domain sources.

Contents

Introduction 5
Olivia: The Facts 6
    Family & Childhood 8
    Early Career 16
    Drivers License & Beyond 22
    Private Life 40
    Everything Else 48
Quotes 59
Olivia: The Lyrics Quiz 68
    Answers 72
Olivia: The Everything Quiz 74
    Answers 78
Wordsearch 81
Crossword Puzzle 82
    Solutions 84

Olivia Rodrigo
INTRODUCTION

Olivia may only be 19 years old, but she's packed a lot into those years! As well as making a name for herself with Disney, she has dominated the last two year's music charts. With hit after hit, and a critically-acclaimed debut album, Olivia is becoming a true superstar!

So how much do you really know about Olivia Rodrigo? *Let's find out!*

THE ULTIMATE OLIVIA RODRIGO FAN BOOK

Olivia Rodrigo
THE FACTS

Where was Olivia born? What do her parents do? How did she become famous?

Let's learn these things and much more about Olivia's childhood, early career, recent achievements and more. Then you can test yourself in our quiz! *Let's get started.*

Olivia Rodrigo
FAMILY & CHILDHOOD

Olivia was born on February 20, 2003, in Murrieta, California, and she is an only child.

• • •

She grew up in Temecula, California where she lived with her parents.

Olivia's full name is Olivia Isabel Rodrigo.

• • •

Her parents are called Sophia and Chris Rodrigo. Her parents are both American, but her background is German-Irish (from her mother's side), while her father is of Filipino descent.

• • •

Olivia's great-grandfather moved from the Philippines to the USA when he was a teenager. Her family still follows Filipino traditions and cuisine at home.

THE ULTIMATE OLIVIA RODRIGO FAN BOOK

"**Try my best but what can I say, all I have is myself at the end of the day.**"

— *All I Want by Olivia Rodrigo*

Olivia's mother is a school teacher and she homeschooled Olivia when she was younger. She also made sure she knew how to play the piano, even though Olivia really hated her piano lessons in the beginning!

• • •

Olivia's father is a therapist.

• • •

Olivia has said that her parents taught her "to be kind and respectful."

Olivia was interested in acting and singing when she was very young. She started classes when she was just six years old.

• • •

Olivia started learning to play guitar when she was 12, which was important for her role on *Bizaardvark*!

• • •

When she started learning the guitar, she also got into songwriting and discovered she was very good at it. *"I remember coming up with melodies and lyrics and writing them down in this pink fluffy notebook that I had won at some arcade. I still keep that notebook on my bedside table."*

> "The scar on my chest is literally from spilling tea that was a little too hot."

— *Olivia Rodrigo*

Olivia attended *Lisa J. Mails Elementary School* and *Dorothy McElhinney Middle School*, where she took part in lots of theater productions.

• • •

Olivia is 5ft 4 inches tall (1.65 meters).

• • •

Her star sign is Pisces. In her social media profiles, Olivia refers to herself as a *'spicy Pisces'*!

• • •

Olivia and her great-grandmother, who lives in Wisconsin, are penpals. They send each other handwritten letters.

THE ULTIMATE OLIVIA RODRIGO FAN BOOK

Olivia Rodrigo
EARLY CAREER

Olivia's first acting job was on an Old Navy commercial.

...

In 2015, Olivia had her first role in a movie playing Grace Thomas in *An American Girl: Grace Stirs Up Success*. It went straight to DVD, but was also shown on the Disney Channel and Netflix several years later.

In An American Girl: Grace Stirs Up Success, Olivia played a talented baker who takes part in a Masterchef competition for young people.

• • •

When Olivia was 13 she landed her first major role as Paige Olvera on the Disney Channel show *Bizaardvark*. When she got the role, she moved with her family to Los Angeles.

• • •

In the show *Bizaardvark*, Olivia's character was a guitarist. She played the role for three seasons from June 2016 until April 2019.

As well as the usual episodes of *Bizaardvark*, the cast also recorded shorter episodes called *Bizaardvark Shorts*.

• • •

After *Bizaardvark*, in 2019, Olivia was cast in another leading role for Disney—Nini Salazar-Roberts in the series *High School Musical: The Musical: The Series*.

• • •

During her time on *High School Musical: The Musical: The Series*, Olivia really got to show off her songwriting talent! She wrote the song *All I Want* and co-wrote *Just for a Moment* with her co-star Joshua Bassett.

THE ULTIMATE OLIVIA RODRIGO FAN BOOK

"
75% of my shirts are my parents' from the 80s and I'm here for it."

— *Olivia Rodrigo*

All I Want was such a successful song that it made it into the American singles charts. This is when people really knew she was a talented singer and songwriter!

• • •

Olivia is contracted to film three seasons of *High School Musical* but has said that her priority now is music.

• • •

In 2017, Olivia had a role in the television series *New Girl*. You can watch her in episode 18 of season 6.

THE ULTIMATE OLIVIA RODRIGO FAN BOOK

Olivia Rodrigo
DRIVERS LICENSE & BEYOND

Olivia was very busy during the COVID-19 pandemic—she started writing a lot of her music during this time, and she also signed her first recording contract with **Interscope** and **Geffen Records**.

In January 2021, Olivia released her first single—*Drivers License*. It was a huge success and reached number one in multiple countries, including the USA.

• • •

Drivers License broke several Spotify records. For one, it was the first song in history to hit 80 million streams in 7 days! It was also 2021's most streamed song globally on Spotify.

• • •

Olivia co-wrote her song *Drivers License* with producer Dan Nigro. He has also helped write music for artists such as Carly Rae Jepson, Kylie Minogue and Lewis Capaldi.

Five months after releasing *Drivers License*, on May 21, 2021, Olivia released her debut album —*Sour*. *Sour* was Spotify's most streamed album globally in 2021!

• • •

One music critic described *Sour* as *"the greatest coming-of-age album since early Taylor Swift or Lorde."* A compliment that we are sure made Olivia very happy!

• • •

Olivia's *Sour* album was originally going to be an EP, with just a few songs, but after the success of her debut single, she added more songs to the album.

THE ULTIMATE OLIVIA RODRIGO FAN BOOK

"**I think I'm good at knowing how people feel, how I feel, and being able to capture that.**"

— *Olivia Rodrigo*

So far, Olivia has released five singles from her *Sour* album, each of which was very successful on the charts. As well as *Drivers License*, she has released *Deja Vu* and *Good 4 U, traitor, happier* and *All I Want*.

• • •

In June 2021, Olivia released a Youtube concert film with a prom theme. It is called *Sour Prom* and is 27 minutes of musical awesomeness.

• • •

As of July 2022, Olivia has already won three Grammy Awards, seven Billboard Music Awards, four MTV Video Music Awards and lots more!

Olivia told W magazine that she felt a huge amount of pressure after the success of *Drivers License*. But it seems like she didn't have to worry!

• • •

When Olivia announced that she was releasing her first single on TikTok, it had 43 million views! Just a few hours later and it was at the top of the charts.

• • •

Having seen the problems that Taylor Swift faced when her record label sold her music masters, Olivia made sure that her recording contract meant she was the owner of her masters. Smart girl!

THE ULTIMATE OLIVIA RODRIGO FAN BOOK

"I think the perspective of a teenage girl is so powerful, and something that doesn't always gets harnessed in its full capacity."

— *Olivia Rodrigo*

Olivia's very successful *Good 4 U* single was written in a sarcastic tone about being happy that an ex-lover is happy without her.

• • •

Olivia performed her song *Drivers License* at the BRIT Awards in London, and it was not only her first-ever awards show performance, but her first time visiting the UK. She posted a photo of herself outside Buckingham Palace on social media.

• • •

Olivia's IMDB profile describes her as: *"a soulful artist with a rare gift for emotive and empathic songwriting."* We would have to agree!

On Twitter, Olivia said that she's most excited to perform her song *Brutal* live.

• • •

Olivia says she has changed since writing *Sour*. *"I remember writing it being so sad and so insecure... but I'm just so far from that now and I'm so proud of that."*

• • •

As she wrote so many songs during lockdown, most of which are not on her album, we're expecting to hear much more amazing music from Olivia in the near future.

Olivia announced her first world tour on December 6, 2021. The *Sour* tour began on April 5, 2022 in Portland, Oregon. The final concert was on July 7th, in London.

• • •

Olivia was named as *Time's* Entertainer of the Year on 9th December, 2021.

• • •

On Christmas Eve, 2021, Olivia uploaded an adorable video of her singing a song she wrote when she was five, called *'The Bels'*.

Olivia's Sour album was the longest reigning number-one album by a female artist in 2021, after spending five weeks at the top spot.

• • •

In 2022, Olivia became the first ever celebrity-partner of the beauty brand *Glossier*.

• • •

During Olivia's concert in Toronto, Canada, Avril Lavigne joined her on the stage to sing the song *Complicated*.

In 2022, Olivia was named Woman of the Year by *Billboard*.

• • •

At the 64th Annual Grammy Awards in 2022, Olivia received seven nominations, and won three awards!

• • •

In March 2022, Olivia released her Disney+ documentary film: *Olivia Rodrigo: Driving Home 2 U*.

THE ULTIMATE OLIVIA RODRIGO FAN BOOK

Olivia Rodrigo
PRIVATE LIFE

Olivia lives a very busy life, but she still finds time to take part in some of her favorite hobbies such as ice skating, swimming, playing piano, and reading.

• • •

In July 2021, Olivia went to the White House and met with President Joe Biden and Vice President Kamala Harris to help promote COVID-19 vaccinations among young people.

During her visit to the White House, Olivia read out funny tweets about vaccines with Dr. Fauci, the President's chief medical advisor. One tweet said: *"Olivia RodriGo to the vaccine clinic."*!

• • •

She also taught Dr. Fauci what 'man-crush Mondays' were! LOL.

• • •

Olivia is a speaker and panelist for the *Geena Davis Institute on Gender in Media*. Gender equality is a cause she feels passionately about.

Olivia dated Ethan Wacker, one of her co-stars on *Bizaardvark* secretly for six months. They announced they were dating in January 2019 on Instagram, but broke up in August that year.

• • •

There were rumors that Olivia was dating her *High School Musical* co-star Joshua Bassett, especially after hearing the lyrics of *Drivers License*! Fans believe the song was about Joshua's new girlfriend Sabrina Carpenter. But neither of them ever confirmed this.

THE ULTIMATE OLIVIA RODRIGO FAN BOOK

My favorite songs are brutally honest and give a vivid look into the artist's life and mind."

— Olivia Rodrigo

Fans also believe that *Deja Vu* may also have been written about Joshua and Sabrina. The song is about an ex who does the same things they did together, but with his new lover.

• • •

Olivia is rumoured (as of July 2022) to be dating Zack Bia. Zack is a 26 year old music executive and DJ. They were first spotted together in April 25 in New York City.

• • •

Olivia's best friend is called Madison.

Olivia is involved with the *She Can STEM* campaign, which encourages girls to study science, technology, engineering, and math.

• • •

Olivia bought her first apartment in 2021, however, she says she still spends a lot of time at her family's home or they come and stay with her.

• • •

When she goes to Starbucks, her go-to order is a tall iced vanilla latte with almond milk.

• • •

Olivia has watched *Twilight* more than 20 times! She's a huge fan. She says, *"something about it always makes me happy."*

THE ULTIMATE OLIVIA RODRIGO FAN BOOK

Olivia Rodrigo
EVERYTHING ELSE

Olivia used her mom's car to make the car sounds you hear in her track *Drivers License*.

• • •

Olivia's Instagram handle is **@olivia.rodrigo**. She already has millions of followers!

Olivia often posts hilarious videos on her TikTok channel. You can follow her at **@livbedumb**.

• • •

Olivia is on Twitter but doesn't post on there very often. She mostly uses it to talk about the causes she is supporting.

• • •

Olivia is a huge fan of Taylor Swift and has said that she is *'The Biggest Swiftie in the Whole World'*.

When Olivia released her single *Drivers License*, Taylor Swift endorsed it on her Instagram account, which was amazing for Olivia.

• • •

Olivia is also a huge fan of New Zealand singer Lorde. Many people compare her music style to Lorde, too.

• • •

When Netflix aired *An American Girl: Grace Stirs Up Success*, Olivia's name was misspelled as Olivo Rodrigo!

THE ULTIMATE OLIVIA RODRIGO FAN BOOK

"

For me, the goal of all music is to take these complicated feelings and externalize them in a way that makes people feel seen."

— *Olivia Rodrigo*

When Olivia was 16 she was a huge fan of Harry Styles and had a cardboard cut out of him!

• • •

Olivia was such a Directioner that she said she used to write One Direction fan fiction when she was in middle school!

• • •

Olivia loves animals but has a fear of birds.

• • •

Niall Horan from One Direction messaged Olivia to give her advice about the music industry.

THE ULTIMATE OLIVIA RODRIGO FAN BOOK

Olivia loves red lipstick. Lots of her social media photos are of her with bright red lips.

• • •

Olivia hasn't yet visited the Philippines, where her father's family are from, but she really wants to.

• • •

Lots of celebrities admire Olivia and her work. Joe Jonas, Hailey Bieber, and TikTok star D'Amelio are just some of Olivia's famous fans!

Our responsibility to protect our planet is as important as ever."

— *Olivia Rodrigo*

Many people think that Olivia is related to model Catriona Gray as they look almost identical! They both have Filipino heritage, but Catriona is Australian.

• • •

On May 11, 2021, Olivia posted a photo of herself with Taylor Swift on her Instagram. She finally got to meet her idol at the 2021 BRIT Awards!

• • •

When asked in a Twitter Q&A what advice she would give to her younger self, she said: *"I would tell her that everything works out the way it is supposed to. I think lil Olivia would be so happy to know all her heartbreak would turn into something really beautiful."*

Olivia's favorite snack of all time is Trader Joe's oatmeal cookies.

• • •

Olivia is an avid reader and regularly recommends books to her fans. You can see her recommendations on her Instagram.

• • •

Olivia's favorite flower is the rose.

• • •

When she goes to Starbucks, her go-to order is a tall iced vanilla latte with almond milk.

Olivia Rodrigo
QUOTES

Olivia is only 19, but she is incredibly smart and is passionate about many important causes.

While she is also silly and makes us laugh, some of her quotes are very inspiring. Here are just a few of our favorites...

"Proud is an understatement. [I'm] lucky to be part of a generation that values not only sustainability for our species but the sanctity of our planet. Let's be the change."

• • •

"So proud of my generation for standing up for our future today and everyday."

• • •

"I try to look as French as possible at all times."

"One girl's trash is another girl's vintage red carpet dress."

• • •

"Small acts of kindness have such a big impact."

• • •

"Quarantine means more writing."

• • •

"Love is everywhere."

"My mom is my shadow."

• • •

"It's really frustrating for me to not be able to convey all of my little intricacies to people right away, especially when it comes to social media."

• • •

"I am the biggest lofthouse cookie stan."

"It's so empowering to see so many people uniting over love and art."

• • •

"Racism in healthcare, specifically reproductive healthcare, is unacceptable."

• • •

"Physics said I was born with a strong desire to love."

THE ULTIMATE OLIVIA RODRIGO FAN BOOK

"**All I did was try my best.**"

— *Olivia Rodrigo*

"Buying clothes second hand is a great way to help the environment! Did you know that fast fashion is the 2nd most polluting industry in the world right under oil?"

. . .

"I love my fairy god parents."

. . .

"I grew up watching Jimmy Fallon every night with my family."

THE ULTIMATE OLIVIA RODRIGO FAN BOOK

Olivia Rodrigo
THE LYRIC QUIZ

Can you name which songs these lyrics are from? It'll be hard, but you got this!

1. *I'd say you broke my heart, but you broke much more than that.*

2. *Remember when you said that you wanted to give me the world?*

3. *I'm the love of your life until I make you mad.*

4. *I made the jokes you tell to her when she's with you.*

5. *I played dumb but I always knew.*

6. *I crossed my heart as you crossed the line.*

7. *I still hear your voice in the traffic.*

8. *I hate to think that I was just your type.*

9. *Brown guilty eyes and little white lies.*

10. *Their win is not my loss.*

11. *Got a pretty face, a pretty boyfriend too.*

12. *Car rides to Malibu.*

13. *I'm selfish, I know.*

14. *Maybe I'm too emotional.*

15. *How could I ever love someone else?*

Answers

How many did you get right?!

1. Enough for You.
2. Good 4 U.
3. 1 Step Forward, 3 Steps Back.
4. Deja Vu.
5. Traitor
6. Favorite Crime.
7. Drivers License.
8. Deja Vu.
9. Traitor.
10. Jealousy, Jealousy.
11. Jealousy, Jealousy.
12. Deja Vu.
13. Happier.
14. Good 4 U.
15. Drivers License.

THE ULTIMATE OLIVIA RODRIGO FAN BOOK

Olivia Rodrigo
THE QUIZ

Now it's time to test your new knowledge on Olivia! You can find the answers on page 78.

1. When was Olivia's single *Deja Vu* released?

2. What is Olivia's favorite flower?

3. What does Olivia like to order at Starbucks?

4. What are Olivia's parents names?

5. What ancestry does her mother have?

6. What was the name of Olivia's character on *Bizaardvark*?

7. When and where did Olivia first meet Taylor Swift?

8. What was Olivia's second single release?

9. What is the name of the song that Olivia wrote for *High School Musical: The Musical: The Series*?

10. Who are Olivia's two main musical influences?

11. Which member of One Direction gave advice to Olivia?

12. What instrument did Olivia's character play in *Bizaardvark*?

13. What is Olivia's mom's job?

14. Where was Olivia born?

15. Olivia has two sisters. True or false?

16. How tall is Olivia?

17. What is Olivia's starsign?

18. What is Olivia's Instagram handle?

19. What was the name of the first movie Olivia starred in?

20. In which year did Olivia sign her first record deal?

21. Olivia visits the Philippines every year. True or false?

22. What was the first stop on Olivia's *Sour* tour?

23. How many singles has Olivia released from her *Sour* album?

24. Which awards did Olivia win at the 2022 Grammys?

Answers

How many did you get right?

1. April 1, 2021.
2. Rose.
3. Tall iced vanilla latte with almond milk
4. Sophia and Chris Rodrigo.
5. German and Irish.
6. Paige Olvera.
7. On May 11, 2021 at the BRIT awards in London.
8. Deja vu.
9. All I Want.
10. Lorde and Taylor Swift.
11. Niall Horan.
12. Guitar.
13. School teacher.
14. Murrieta, California
15. False. She is an only child.
16. 5ft 4 inches tall (1.65 meters)
17. Pisces.
18. @olivia.rodrigo.
19. An American Girl: Grace Stirs Up Success
20. 2020.
21. False.
22. Portland, Oregon.
23. Five.
24. Best New Artist, Best Pop Vocal Album for Sour, and Best Pop Solo Performance for Drivers License

Olivia Rodrigo
WORD SEARCH

R	T	E	A	Z	T	V	D	S	E	J	G
S	O	U	R	R	P	R	T	E	S	F	T
W	A	L	D	G	H	S	A	N	G	D	R
M	U	S	I	C	I	W	Y	I	D	W	E
R	E	A	S	V	L	G	L	N	T	S	S
F	D	L	A	S	I	F	O	I	E	O	D
H	G	L	D	S	P	A	R	S	D	F	R
H	G	I	D	S	P	W	S	E	I	D	O
J	H	W	D	S	I	E	W	Q	S	S	I
M	N	A	Z	Z	N	R	I	H	N	W	T
P	U	N	J	K	E	D	F	G	E	A	E
X	S	T	X	R	S	G	T	D	Y	C	A

Can you find all the words below in the wordsearch puzzle on the left?

OLIVIA	DISNEY	NINI
PHILIPPINES	MUSIC	ALL I WANT
SOUR	TRAITOR	TAYLOR SWIFT

Olivia Rodrigo
CROSSWORD PUZZLE

Across

6. Starsign.
9. Fourth single.
11. Hometown.

Down

1. Mother's name.
3. First TV commercial.
5. Disney show.
7. First album.
8. Character on Bizaardvark.
10. Number of Grammy Awards.

THE ULTIMATE OLIVIA RODRIGO FAN BOOK

SOLUTIONS

					T				
S	O	U	R		P	R			
	L				H	A	N		
M	U	S	I	C	I		Y	I	
	A		V		L		L	N	T
	L		I		O	I			O
	L			P	A	R		D	R
	I			P		S		I	
	W			I		W		S	
	A			N		I		N	
	N			E		F		E	
	T			S		T		Y	

Can't get enough?!

Visit us at
www.bellanovabooks.com
for more fun celebrity books.

TAYLOR SWIFT
THE ULTIMATE FAN BOOK 2022/3

BILLIE EILISH
THE ULTIMATE FAN BOOK

HARRY STYLES

www.ingramcontent.com/pod-product-compliance
Lightning Source LLC
LaVergne TN
LVHW050135080526
838202LV00061B/6491